**TITLE: The Untapped Secrets Of Influence: Delve Into the Expanded Psychology Of Persuasion**

**KEITH A. SPERRY**

# Table Of Contents

INTRODUCTION_____3

CHAPTER 1
DEFINITION OF IMPORTANT TERMS_____8

CHAPTER 2
LEADERSHIP ◼ INFLUENCE _____20

Chapter 3
THE PSYCHOLOGY OF INFLUENCE_____31

CHAPTER 4
THE ART OF INFLUENCE _____37

CHAPTER 5
INFLUENCING OTHERS_____43

CHAPTER 6
INFLUENCING IN DIFFERENT CONTEXTS___ 29

CHAPTER 7
BECOMING AN INFLUENTIAL PERSON_____ 39

CONCLUSION_____ 43

# INTRODUCTION

There was once a little village hidden in a valley surrounded by lofty mountains. The villagers lived in harmony and peace, but they had a problem: their crops were not yielding enough food to sustain them throughout the year. They had tried everything they could think of, but the harsh climate and poor soil made it difficult to grow enough food.

One day, a wise man from a neighboring village came to visit the village. He was known for his great wisdom and his ability to solve difficult problems. The villagers welcomed him warmly and asked him for his advice on how they could improve their crops.

The wise man spent several days observing the village and the surrounding landscape.

He talked to the villagers and learned about their struggles. Then, he came up with a plan. He suggested that the villagers build a system of canals to bring water from a nearby river to their fields.

The villagers were skeptical. They had never heard of such a thing before, and they were afraid it would be too expensive and difficult to build. But the wise man was persuasive. He explained how the canals would bring much-needed water to their fields and increase their crop yields. He showed them how it had worked in other villages and how it could work for them.

Slowly but surely, the wise man began to influence the villagers. He talked to them one-on-one and in small groups. He listened to their concerns and addressed them one by one. He framed the canals as a solution to their problems and reframed their objections as opportunities to make the plan better.Soon, the villagers began to see the benefits of the plan. They started to work together to build the canals.

They overcame obstacles and setbacks, but they kept going. They trusted the wise man's advice and persevered.In the end, the canals were built, and the village flourished. The crops grew taller and stronger than ever before. The villagers had enough food to sustain them throughout the year, and they even had enough to sell to neighboring villages. They were no longer struggling to survive, but thriving.The wise man had used his influence to help the villagers solve their problem. He had listened to them, understood their concerns, and found a solution that worked for them. He had used his persuasion skills to convince them to take action and overcome their doubts.

From that day on, the villagers respected the wise man and sought his advice on other matters. They had learned the power of influence and how it could be used for the greater good. They had learned that by working together and trusting each other, they could achieve great things.

And the wise man? He continued on his journey, helping other villages and spreading his wisdom. He knew that influence was not just about getting people to do what you want, but about helping them achieve their goals and become their best selves. And that, he knew, was the greatest benefit of all.

# CHAPTER 1

# DEFINITION OF IMPORTANT TERMS

## What is influence?

Influence is the ability to shape the attitudes, beliefs, behaviors, and decisions of others. It is the power to persuade or guide others towards a particular outcome, whether that is a change in behavior, a shift in perspective, or a decision to take a specific action. Influence can be positive or negative, intentional or unintentional, and can occur in a variety of contexts, including personal relationships, social groups, organizations, and society as a whole.

There are many factors that contribute to influence. One important factor is credibility. People are more likely to be influenced by someone they perceive as credible and trustworthy. Credibility can come from expertise, experience, or reputation, among other factors. Another factor is likability. People are more likely to be influenced by someone they like or admire. This can come from shared interests, values, or personality traits.

Influence can also be influenced by social dynamics. People tend to conform to the opinions and behaviors of others in their social group, in a phenomenon known as social proof. Social proof can be powerful in shaping attitudes and behaviors, particularly in situations where people are uncertain or unclear about the appropriate course of action.

Influence can also be influenced by the way messages are presented. Persuasive communication techniques such as emotional appeals, social norms, and scarcity can be used to increase the effectiveness of a message and its influence on others. Additionally, the timing and context of a message can also impact its influence, as people are more receptive to certain messages at certain times or in certain situations.

Influence can be used for a variety of purposes, including promoting positive social change, selling products or services, or gaining support for a particular cause or agenda. It is important to use influence ethically and responsibly, and to consider the potential consequences of the outcomes being sought. Ultimately, influence is a powerful tool that can be used to achieve important goals and make a positive impact in the world.

## Why is it important?

Influence is important for a variety of reasons, both on an individual and societal level. Here are a few reasons why influence matters:

- Achieving personal and professional goals: Influence can help individuals achieve their personal and professional goals. By influencing others, individuals can gain support for their ideas, persuade others to take a particular action, or build relationships and alliances that can help them achieve their goals.

- Building social connections: Influence can help individuals build and maintain social connections. By being influential, individuals can gain the respect and admiration of others, which can lead to stronger relationships and social networks.

- Promoting positive social change: Influence can be used to promote positive social change by raising awareness of important issues, changing attitudes and beliefs, and inspiring action. By being influential, individuals and organizations can drive social progress and make a positive impact in the world.

- Advancing careers and businesses: Influence can be an important factor in advancing careers and businesses. By being influential, individuals and organizations can gain credibility, build trust, and establish themselves as leaders in their field, which can lead to new opportunities and increased success.

- Strengthening communities and societies: Influence can be used to strengthen communities and societies by promoting cooperation, collaboration, and positive social norms. By being influential, individuals and organizations can inspire others to work together towards common goals, and to support positive behaviors and attitudes.

Overall, influence is important because it can help individuals and organizations achieve their goals, build relationships, promote positive social change, advance careers and businesses, and strengthen communities and societies. By understanding the factors that contribute to influence and using it ethically and responsibly, individuals and organizations can make a positive impact in the world.

## Types of influence

There are various types of influence that can shape the attitudes, beliefs, and behaviors of individuals and groups. Here are a few examples:

- Social influence: This type of influence refers to the way individuals and groups conform to the opinions and behaviors of others in their social group. Social influence can be positive or negative, and can take many forms, including peer pressure, social norms, and groupthink. Imagine a group of teenagers who are all wearing a certain type of clothing or listening to a particular type of music because it's popular among their peers. They may feel pressure to conform to these social norms in order to fit in and avoid being ostracized.

- Expert influence: This type of influence comes from individuals who are seen as experts in their field. Expert influence is based on the perception of the individual's knowledge, skills, and experience, and can be used to persuade others to adopt certain beliefs or behaviors. A doctor who is promoting the benefits of a particular type of medication may use their medical credentials and expertise to persuade patients to try the medication. Patients may be more likely to trust the doctor's recommendation due to their perceived expertise in the field.

- Emotional influence: This type of influence comes from the emotional appeals that are used to persuade individuals. Emotional influence can take many forms, including fear, anger, sadness, or joy, and can be used to elicit a particular response or behavior. For instance, A political campaign may use emotional appeals to persuade voters to support a particular candidate. For example, a campaign ad may show images of children in poverty or elderly people struggling to afford healthcare, in order to elicit feelings of compassion and empathy and motivate voters to support policies that address these issues.

- Authority influence: This type of influence comes from individuals who hold positions of authority or power. Authority influence can be based on the perceived legitimacy of the individual's position, or on the use of coercive power to influence the behavior of others. A police officer who is directing traffic at an intersection may use their authority to direct drivers to stop or go, and drivers may obey their commands out of respect for their position of authority.

- Ideological influence: This type of influence comes from individuals or groups who promote a particular ideology or worldview. Ideological influence can be used to shape attitudes and beliefs, and to promote certain behaviors or actions. A perfect example of ideological influence is a religious leader who promotes a particular set of values or beliefs and may use their influence to persuade their followers to adopt these beliefs and values. For example, a preacher may use their sermons to promote the importance of forgiveness and compassion as core values of their religion.

- Cultural influence: This type of influence comes from the values, beliefs, and traditions of a particular culture or society. Cultural influence can shape attitudes and behaviors, and can be used to promote certain social norms or practices. A person who is raised in a particular culture may adopt the values, beliefs, and behaviors of that culture. For example, a person from a culture that values punctuality may prioritize being on time for appointments and meetings, while a person from a culture that values relaxation and leisure may prioritize taking time off work to spend with friends and family.

By understanding these different types of influence, individuals and organizations can better understand how to influence others and achieve their goals.

# CHAPTER 2

## LEADERSHIP ■ INFLUENCE

There's a thin line between leadership and influence, they go hand in hand which is to say that you can't have one without the other and still be effective. Here's what I mean;

Leadership and influence are often closely related concepts, but there is a subtle difference between the two. Leadership can be defined as the ability to inspire, motivate, and guide others to achieve a common goal or vision, while influence refers to the ability to affect or persuade others to change their attitudes, beliefs, or behaviors.

In other words, leadership is about guiding a group of people towards a common objective, while influence is about shaping the beliefs and actions of individuals or groups. However, leadership often involves using influence to achieve goals, and influence can be a key component of effective leadership.

For example, a leader may use their influence to persuade team members to adopt new ideas or processes, or to motivate them to work harder towards a shared goal. Similarly, a leader may use their position of authority to influence the decision-making of others, or to shape the culture and values of an organization. So you cannot lead without the power to influence and you can't influence effectively if you don't posses the skills of leadership.

However, there is a risk that influence can be used for personal gain, without regard for the needs or interests of others. In this case, influence can become a form of manipulation or coercion, rather than a tool for effective leadership.

Overall, the line between leadership and influence can be thin, and effective leaders must understand how to use their influence in a positive and ethical way to guide and motivate others towards shared goals.

## Basic skills of leadership

The basic skills of leadership can be simplified into three main categories:

- Communication: Effective leaders need to be able to communicate their vision, goals, and expectations clearly and persuasively to their team. This includes not just verbal communication, but also active listening and nonverbal communication skills.

- Relationship-building: Good leaders build strong relationships with their team members and create a positive work culture. This involves being approachable, empathetic, and respectful, and taking the time to understand the needs and perspectives of each team member.

- Decision-making: Leaders need to be able to make informed decisions that are in the best interest of their team and the organization as a whole. This involves gathering and analyzing data, considering different perspectives, and taking decisive action when necessary.

Other important skills for leadership include problem-solving, delegation, strategic thinking, and emotional intelligence. Effective leaders are also able to inspire and motivate their team, set clear goals and expectations, and provide constructive feedback and support to help their team members grow and develop.

While leadership skills can take time and practice to develop, the basic skills of communication, relationship-building, and decision-making provide a strong foundation for effective leadership.

## The keys of influence

Here are three main keys to influence:

1.  Build trust: One of the most important keys to influence is building trust with the people you are trying to influence. People are more likely to be influenced by someone they trust and respect. Be honest, upfront, and consistent in your behaviors and communication to develop trust. Be reliable, keep your promises, and show empathy and understanding.

2.  Understand your audience: To be influential, you need to understand the needs, wants, and motivations of the people you are trying to influence. This requires active listening and

empathy. Try to see things from their perspective and tailor your message to their interests and concerns. Use language and examples that resonate with them and address their specific needs.

3. Be persuasive: Finally, to be influential, you need to be persuasive. This means presenting your ideas in a compelling and convincing way. Use evidence and logical arguments to support your ideas, and appeal to the emotions of your audience. Use storytelling, metaphors, and vivid imagery to bring your message to life. Be confident and passionate, but also respectful and open to feedback.

By building trust, understanding your audience, and being persuasive, you can increase your influence and achieve your goals more effectively. These keys to influence apply in many different contexts, from personal relationships to professional settings and beyond.

## Sources of influence

The sources of influence can vary depending on the context and situation, but here are some common sources of influence:

- Expertise: People who have specialized knowledge or skills in a particular area are often seen as authoritative and influential.

- Authority: People in positions of power or authority, such as managers, politicians, or religious leaders, can exert influence based on their position.

- Relationships: People who are well-liked, respected, or admired can have a strong influence on others through their social connections and networks.

- Persuasive communication: People who are skilled communicators and can present their ideas in a convincing way can influence others to adopt their perspective or take a particular action.

- Social proof: People tend to look to others to determine the appropriate behavior in a particular situation, so those who are seen as popular, successful, or knowledgeable can have a strong influence on others.

- Incentives: Offering rewards or punishments can influence people to behave in a particular way or adopt a particular belief.

- Scarcity: People tend to value things that are rare or hard to obtain, so limiting access to something can make it more desirable and influential.

- Consistency and commitment: People tend to follow through on commitments they have made, so getting someone to make a small commitment can increase the likelihood that they will make a larger commitment later on.

These are just a few examples of sources of influence, and there may be others depending on the context and situation. Understanding these sources of influence can help individuals and organizations develop effective strategies for influencing others and achieving their goals.

# CHAPTER 3

# THE PSYCHOLOGY OF INFLUENCE

The psychology of influence is the study of how people are influenced by others and the factors that affect their decision-making. It is based on the premise that people are often unaware of the influences that shape their thoughts, beliefs, and behaviors, and that these influences can be harnessed to persuade or motivate individuals to take specific actions.

Some important factors that can influence human behavior include liking, scarcity, social proof, consistency, commitment etc. Understanding these factors and how they can be leveraged to influence others is a key component of the psychology of influence.

Overall, the psychology of influence is a complex and multifaceted field that draws on insights from psychology, sociology, marketing, and other disciplines to understand how people make decisions and how those decisions can be influenced. By understanding the psychology of influence, individuals and organizations can improve their ability to persuade and motivate others, and achieve their goals more effectively.

# The Principles Of Persuasion

The principles of persuasion can be summarized as follows:

Reciprocity - give and take,

Social proof - influence from others,

Authority - deference to experts,

Consistency and commitment - staying true to oneself,

Liking - influencing through rapport,

Scarcity - importance of limited resources.

# Cognitive biases and heuristics

Cognitive biases and heuristics are mental shortcuts that people use to make decisions and judgments. These mental shortcuts can be useful in certain situations, as they allow individuals to make quick decisions without having to analyze every piece of information. However, they can also lead to errors in judgment and decision-making, as they may result in individuals overlooking important information or making faulty assumptions.

Some common cognitive biases and heuristics include:

- Confirmation bias - the tendency to seek out information that confirms our existing beliefs, and to discount information that contradicts those beliefs.

- Anchoring bias - the tendency to rely too heavily on the first piece of information we receive when making a decision, even if that information is not particularly relevant or accurate.

- Availability heuristic - the tendency to overestimate the importance of information that is readily available to us, and to underestimate the importance of information that is less accessible.

- Framing effect - the way information is presented can have a significant impact on how people perceive and respond to it.

- Overconfidence bias - the tendency to overestimate one's own abilities, knowledge, or judgment, and to underestimate the likelihood of making errors.

- Hindsight bias - the tendency to believe, after an event has occurred, that one would have predicted or anticipated the outcome.

Understanding cognitive biases and heuristics is important, as it can help individuals to make more informed decisions and avoid making common errors in judgment. By recognizing the ways in which our minds may be biased, we can take steps to mitigate those biases and make more accurate, rational decisions.

## The power of social proof

Social proof is a powerful force that can shape our behavior and influence our decision-making in ways we may not even realize. From the clothes we wear to the products we buy, we often look to the actions and opinions of others to guide our own choices. By understanding the power of social proof, we can harness its potential to persuade and influence others, and to create positive change in our own lives and in the world around us.

# CHAPTER 4

# THE ART OF INFLUENCE

The art of influence is the ability to persuade and motivate others to take a particular course of action, whether that be through the use of logical arguments, emotional appeals, or other tactics. It requires a deep understanding of human psychology and behavior, as well as the ability to communicate effectively and build rapport with others. Those who master the art of influence can inspire others to achieve their goals, overcome obstacles, and create positive change in the world.

## Developing Rapport And Trust

Developing rapport and trust is a crucial aspect of building strong relationships and influencing others. It involves creating a sense of connection and mutual understanding between yourself and the other person, and establishing a foundation of trust that allows for open and honest communication.

You can develop rapport and trust by being authentic and consistent in your commitments.

By developing rapport and trust with others, you can build strong relationships that allow you to influence and motivate them in positive ways. Whether you're working with colleagues, leading a team, or trying to persuade others to support a particular cause, the ability to create meaningful connections and build trust is essential to achieving your goals.

## Active Listening And Empathy

Active listening involves fully focusing on the other person, paying attention to their words and demonstrating that you are engaged. Empathy involves putting yourself in the other person's shoes, understanding their perspective, and demonstrating that you care about them. These skills are essential for effective communication and building strong relationships.

# Framing And Reframing

Framing and reframing are techniques used in communication to shape the way people perceive information or ideas.

Framing involves presenting information in a way that emphasizes certain aspects of it and de-emphasizes others. It can be used to make information more persuasive, by highlighting its relevance and importance, or to appeal to people's emotions by framing information in a way that is relatable to their experiences.

Reframing involves changing the way information is presented to shift the meaning and perspective. It can be used to challenge assumptions or biases, by presenting information in a way that challenges people's preconceptions. Reframing can also be used to create new possibilities and perspectives, by looking at a situation from a different angle.

Both framing and reframing can be powerful tools for influencing and persuading others. By carefully choosing how information is presented and framed, communicators can create a more compelling and persuasive message, and increase their chances of success.

In short, Framing and reframing are communication techniques used to shape how people perceive information or ideas. Framing emphasizes certain aspects, while reframing changes the meaning and perspective. These tools can be used to influence and persuade others by creating a more compelling and persuasive message.

# Effective Communication Skills

Effective communication skills include active listening, clarity, empathy, nonverbal communication, respect, feedback, and flexibility. These skills are essential for building relationships, resolving conflicts, and achieving success in personal and professional contexts.

# CHAPTER 5

# INFLUENCING OTHERS

## The importance of understanding the other person

Understanding the other person is critical to the process of influencing them. When we understand the other person's perspectives, motivations, and values, we can tailor our communication and influence strategies in a way that is more likely to resonate with them.

By taking the time to understand the other person, we can identify their needs and concerns, and present our ideas and proposals in a way that addresses those needs and concerns. This can increase the chances of the other person being receptive to our message, and can make them more likely to take action based on our influence. Additionally, understanding the other person can help to build rapport and trust, which are essential components of effective influence. When we demonstrate that we understand and respect the other person's point of view, they are more likely to view us as credible and trustworthy, and more willing to listen to what we have to say.

Overall, understanding the other person is a critical component of effective influence, as it enables us to communicate in a way that is more meaningful, persuasive, and respectful, and increases the chances of a successful outcome.

Strategies for Getting Others to say Yes!

If you must influence others or if you have learnt the principles of influence, people should find it hard to say no to your proposals. There are several effective strategies for getting others to say yes, including:

- Reciprocity: Offering something of value to the other person first, which increases the likelihood that they will reciprocate by saying yes to our request.

- Social proof: Demonstrating that others have already said yes to our request, which creates a sense of social pressure and increases the likelihood that the other person will follow suit.

- Consistency: Emphasizing that the other person has already expressed agreement or commitment to related ideas or values, which makes it more likely that they will say yes to our request in order to maintain consistency.

- Authority: Establishing credibility and expertise in the relevant area, which increases the perceived legitimacy and persuasiveness of our request.

- Scarcity: Emphasizing the limited availability or opportunity of what we are offering, which creates a sense of urgency and increases the perceived value of saying yes.

By using these strategies, we can increase the likelihood of getting others to say yes to our requests and influence their behavior in a positive way. However, it's important to use these strategies ethically and respectfully, and to prioritize the other person's needs and interests in the process of persuasion.

## Overcoming Resistance And Objections

Meanwhile, there are times when people will resist or say no to us. Overcoming resistance and objections is an important aspect of effective influence and persuasion. Here are some strategies that can be used:

- Acknowledge the objection: Showing that we understand and respect the other person's concerns and objections can help to build rapport and trust, and increase their receptiveness to our message.

- Reframe the objection: Reframing the objection in a positive light or from a different perspective can help to address the underlying concerns and make it easier for the other person to say yes.

- Provide evidence or social proof: Providing evidence or examples that support our message can help to overcome objections and increase the perceived legitimacy and persuasiveness of our request.

- Address underlying needs and interests: Understanding the other person's underlying needs and interests can help to identify alternative solutions that address their concerns and objections while still achieving our desired outcome.

- Use humor or storytelling: Using humor or storytelling can help to build rapport, diffuse tension, and increase the other person's receptiveness to our message.

- Offer incentives: Offering incentives or rewards can help to overcome objections and increase the perceived value of saying yes to our request.

By using these strategies, we can overcome resistance and objections and increase the chances of successfully influencing others in a positive way. However, it's important to use these strategies ethically and respectfully, and to prioritize the other person's needs and interests in the process of persuasion.

Okay, imagine this scenario;

Sarah is an MLM seller who is trying to convince her friend, Emily, to join her downline and start selling products as well. Emily is hesitant because she's heard negative things about MLMs and doesn't want to risk losing money.

To overcome Emily's objections, Sarah first acknowledges her concerns and shows that she understands where she's coming from. She says, "I totally get it, Emily. MLMs have gotten a bad reputation because of some bad actors out there. But I want to assure you that the company I work with is reputable and has a great track record."

Next, Sarah reframes Emily's objection in a positive light. By telling her that she understands her fear to lose her money, she continues by explaining how the opportunity has the potential to help her earn significantly higher than her traditional job. "Plus, the products we sell are really high-quality and I think you'll love them." She says.

Sarah also provides social proof by sharing stories of other people who have joined her downline and have been successful with the company. She says, "I have a friend who started out just like you, and now she's making a full-time income and loving her job. I think you could have similar success if you give it a chance."

Finally, Sarah addresses Emily's underlying needs and interests by offering to provide training and support to help her succeed in the business. She says, "I'll be there every step of the way to help you build your business and make sure you're successful. I believe in you and I know you can do this."

By using these strategies, Sarah is able to overcome Emily's objections and persuade her to join her downline. However, it's important to note that MLMs can be controversial and it's important to thoroughly research and evaluate any potential business opportunity before making a decision.

Using Persuasion Ethically

Persuasion can be used ethically by respecting the other person's autonomy, being transparent and truthful, avoiding manipulation, and focusing on shared values and interests. It's important to prioritize the well-being and best interests of the other person, rather than just trying to get them to do what you want. So don't just go around beating your chest that everyone who hears you will believe you. Come out of it because even Jesus was doubted. When you try to do that, you are practically trying to force them and people try their hardest to resist a forceful influencer. Pay attention to the other person's needs and wellbeing, also remember their personal space so you don't cross your boundaries.

# CHAPTER 6

# INFLUENCING IN DIFFERENT CONTEXTS

## Influence In The Workplace

Influence in the workplace is the ability to persuade others to take certain actions or adopt certain beliefs. It's a crucial skill for leaders and managers, as well as anyone who wants to be successful in their career. The keys to influence include building rapport and trust, active listening and empathy, effective communication skills, understanding others' perspectives, and using persuasion ethically. Learn the strategies for influence as outlined in this book, By using influence effectively and ethically, individuals can achieve their goals and help their organizations succeed.

## Influence In Personal Relationships

To influence in personal relationships, it's important to build rapport and trust, actively listen and show empathy, communicate effectively, and understand the other person's perspective. It's also important to use persuasion ethically by respecting the other person's autonomy and focusing on shared values and interests. By using these skills and strategies, individuals can strengthen their personal relationships and achieve their goals in a positive and respectful manner. Know when to let go and be transparent in all you do with wisdom.

## Influence In Negotiations

Influence is a critical skill in negotiations, as it allows individuals to persuade others to accept a certain outcome or proposal. Key tactics for influencing in negotiations include active listening and empathy, effective communication, understanding the other party's interests and perspective, and building rapport and trust. Using social proof, framing and reframing, and addressing objections and resistance can also be effective in negotiations. It's important to use influence ethically and strive for win-win outcomes that benefit all parties involved. By mastering the art of influence in negotiations, individuals can achieve better outcomes and strengthen their relationships with others.

Influence in politics and public speaking

Influence plays an important role in politics and public speaking, as it enables individuals to persuade the public and gain support for their ideas or causes. Effective communication, the use of compelling stories and anecdotes, establishing credibility and authority, and engaging with the audience are some of the key strategies for influence in these areas. Social proof and other persuasion techniques can also be useful. However, it's important to use influence ethically and avoid manipulating or deceiving the public. By mastering the art of influence in politics and public speaking, individuals can effectively communicate their message and drive positive change.

# CHAPTER 7

# BECOMING AN INFLUENTIAL PERSON

I always tell people that to become an influencer, you have to first of all look at the influencial people you have encountered or heard of, study their personal characteristics as well as their habits, then you develop your own style. Now on a generql note, let's look at them in details.

# Personal characteristics of influential people

There are several personal characteristics that influential people often possess:

1. Confidence: They exude a sense of self-assurance and conviction in their beliefs and ideas.

2. Empathy: They have the ability to understand and connect with others, which allows them to build rapport and trust.

3. Charisma: They possess a natural charm and appeal that draws people towards them.

4. Adaptability: They can adapt their communication style and approach to fit different situations and audiences.

5. Resilience: They are able to overcome setbacks and failures and persist in the pursuit of their goals.

6. Integrity: They are honest, transparent, and consistent in their values and actions.

7. Vision: They have a clear vision of what they want to achieve and can articulate it effectively to others.

By cultivating these personal characteristics, individuals can become more influential and effective in their interactions with others.

## Habits Of Influential People

Here are some habits of influential people:

1. Continuous learning: They are always seeking to expand their knowledge and skills.

2. Networking: They cultivate a strong network of connections and build relationships with others.

3. Listening: They are skilled at active listening, which allows them to understand and empathize with others.

4. Positive attitude: They maintain a positive attitude and outlook, which helps them overcome challenges and setbacks.

5. Taking action: They are not afraid to take action and make decisions, even in the face of uncertainty or risk.

6. Goal setting: They set clear goals and develop plans to achieve them.

7. Adaptability: They are adaptable and can adjust to changing circumstances or situations.

8. Consistency: They are consistent in their actions and behaviors, which helps build trust and credibility with others.

# Developing Your Own Influence Style

Developing your own style of influence involves a process of self-discovery and self-awareness, followed by deliberate practice and refinement. Here are some steps you can take:

1. Identify your strengths and weaknesses: Reflect on your own personality, communication style, and values. Consider what makes you unique and how you can leverage those qualities in your interactions with others.

2. Define your goals: Determine what you want to achieve through your influence, whether it's building relationships, achieving a specific outcome, or inspiring others to action.

3. Study different influence styles: Learn about different influence styles and techniques, such as emotional appeal, logic and reason, or social proof. Consider which ones align with your goals and strengths.

4. Practice and refine: Experiment with different influence techniques and styles in a variety of situations. Seek feedback from others and evaluate your own performance. Continuously refine and adapt your approach to fit different contexts and audiences.

5. Build credibility and trust: Develop a reputation for honesty, integrity, and reliability. Consistently deliver on your promises and maintain open and transparent communication with others.

6. Embrace authenticity: Stay true to yourself and your values. Don't try to mimic

someone else's influence style or approach. Instead, focus on developing your own unique voice and perspective.

By following these steps and staying committed to continuous self-improvement, you can develop your own authentic and effective style of influence. Above all, Maintain integrity and authenticity while being influential.

# CHAPTER 8

# CONCLUSION

## Review Of Key Points And Final Thoughts

The book on influence covers a wide range of topics related to how to influence others.

1. Influence is the ability to persuade or convince others to take a certain course of action.

2. There are different types of influence, including personal, social, and organizational.

3. Key skills for influencing include active listening, empathy, framing and reframing, and effective communication.

4. Successful influencers often have personal characteristics such as confidence, empathy, and a growth mindset.

5. Ethical influence involves using persuasion to benefit both parties, rather than just oneself.

6. In the workplace, influence is often used for collaboration, team building, and leadership.

7. In personal relationships, influence can be used to strengthen connections and resolve conflicts.

8. In negotiations and public speaking, influence can be used to persuade and communicate effectively.

9. Developing your own style of influence involves identifying your strengths and weaknesses, defining your goals, studying different influence styles, practicing and refining, building credibility and trust, and embracing authenticity.

Influence is a powerful tool that can be used to achieve both personal and professional success. By developing key skills such as active listening, empathy, effective communication, and framing and reframing, individuals can become more persuasive and influential in their interactions with others. However, it's important to use influence ethically and for the benefit of all parties involved. Successful influencers often have personal characteristics such as confidence, empathy, and a growth mindset. Developing your own style of influence requires practice, self-reflection, and a willingness to adapt and refine your approach over time. Ultimately, by understanding the principles of influence and mastering the skills and habits of influential people, individuals can achieve their goals and make a positive impact on the world around them.